Gallery Books
Editor Peter Fallon

SPINDRIFT

Vona Groarke

SPINDRIFT

Gallery Books

Spindrift
is first published
simultaneously in paperback
and in a clothbound edition
on 17 September 2009.

The Gallery Press
Loughcrew
Oldcastle
County Meath
Ireland

www.gallerypress.com

ISBN 978 1 85235 475 6 *paperback*
978 1 85235 476 3 *clothbound*

A CIP catalogue record for this book
is available from the British Library.

Contents

spindrift, n. spray blown from the crests of waves by the wind
— *Oxford Dictionary of English*

Some Weather

Among the things
(though these are not things)
I did to pre-empt the storm were:
upturn, stow, disconnect,
shut down, shutter, shut.

But, while the house sulked,
the sky scolded
and I observed an hour's breadth,
the storm tossed out its tinsmith verbs
somewhat to the west.

The Jetty

Summer-bleached and swaddling the paddle-boat
and tin canoe, the jetty shoulders, for a moment,
clean right angles, lichen seams heavy as voices
tacking now across water, calling 'Don't' or 'Boat' —
it hardly matters to me. The way I scribble
is like the way a squirrel or a cardinal
is fumbling in the thicket to my left:
at least he knows what he's looking for.
I think I've found it when the opposite hill
throws down another version of itself
on the lake's gloss. Soon the evening
will soak boat and jetty; eventually, this page.
By then I'll have slipped inside a fuchsia bud
of wine and spindle tips of light from a porch
over the lake that answers, very nicely, to our own.

Sleepless

The humdrum of cicadas
is like white noise on a radio
I last tuned to *Mo Cheol Thú*.

*

The fridge motor turns over
like the engine of a great ship
hauling me out to the spot in the ocean
that's just as far from one home as the other.

*

A borrowed cellphone
charges and dims on the floor beside me
like a spray of fireflies shaken out
of a second-hand ash tree.

Away

We have our own smallholding:
persimmon tree, crawl space, stoop,
red earth basement, ceiling fans, a job.

Hours I'm not sure where I am,
flitting through every amber
between Gales and Drumcliffe Road.

I paint woodwork the exact azure
of a wave's flipside
out the back of Spiddal pier

and any given morning pins
a swatch of sunlight
to my purple shamrock plant.

My faithless heart ratchets
in time to slower vowels,
higher daylight hours.

I grow quiet. Yesterday
I answered in a class of Irish
at the checkout of Walgreen's.

I walk through the day-to-day
as if ferrying a pint glass
filled to the brim with water

that spills into my own accent:
pewtered, dim, far-reaching,
lost for words.

The Small Hours

A joyrider rips up Lockland.
It takes barely five minutes
for a Precinct helicopter
to dip and swivel over lawns
and two opposing lines of cars
parked innocently snug to the sidewalk.
They haven't found him yet.
Every couple of minutes or so
my blind soaks in outrageous light
and the helicopter hauls its drone
and feud all over my backyard.
There's a fan over my bed
that says similar things in summer:
adages, reproach and rhetoric.
I talk too much; give far too much away.
In mumbling my company I reckon on
a two-fold pay-off: some echo;
being found out, consequence.
I lie low. Minutes swell.
He must be out there somewhere,
lights switched off, crouched and bundled,
foot within an inch of the get-go.
I pull the comforter up over my ears,
count to forty-two, then start over.
I'm trying, hard and fast, to hold my breath.

An American Jay

Midterm, and the kids hang round like wisps of summer,
spinning channels between the election and Iraq,
laughing only at ads for the new Hummer

dealership on Silas or Larry Cobalt's Rent-a-Wreck
or the pre-Thanksgiving clear-out at K-Mart.
Even the radio doubts the space between a rock

and a hard place on the war front. It launches in on Marx
which is round about the point where I switch, finally,
to an Anglophile mid-morning with the Kumars

or *All Creatures Great and Small* or *The Royle Family*
or any other one of a hundred ways to fritter
a tea-break or two on what's billed, not funnily

enough, as Classic Hour. But not even the future
tense of wheatfields in Ohio or plain-speak in Kansas
can pull us away from a pre-paid, half-hour feature

on William Carlos Williams reading 'Queen Anne's
Lace', a recording that sheds decades and darkness
as ripe as this Fall's haws or quinces

left to rot on the ground for lack of a crew to harvest
even this sound-bite. Two experts pull rank (or
what you will) on this morning's conversational largesse.

They're at it hammer and tongs, spite and rancour
name-calling, the works. I turn off, compose
myself in the back bedroom for the crankier

exercise of the afternoon's hour on campus
during which I'll try to praise and encourage
my nine students to find some new compass

that points beyond the fashionable entourage
of sentimental dudes and soulful sidekicks
who plan on moving, after May, to Anchorage

to finish novels, waitress, work as psychics
in the packed-ice atmosphere of a northern funfair
with its stoical rides and half-hearted high jinks.

But for now they're stuck with my unfair
insistence on their coming up with a ballad
of sorts for next Tuesday. I give good build-up, fanfare

and blow, Keats and Goldsmith, the full absurd ballet
of merciless broads, mad dogs and Englishmen, all equally
metered, fastened to a narrative of this week's ballot

or a news report of something local: spinach and e-coli,
Jerry Swaim, plucked from his job in a Raleigh abattoir,
to serenade the First Lady with Rat Pack classics on his ukulele.

I hand out clippings. A check-out girl in CVS is an avatar.
A preacher is arrested for an international drugs deal.
The Warthogs ballpark is declared too amateur.

Sue Zeller advises strongly against Drink and Dial.
Op-eds address the Presidential lack of hard headlines.
Nimrod's has a lunchtime special on tikka and dhal.

My students smirk. I'm square. Fixed in the headlights
of form and tradition, I tell them, 'Next, it's an ode'.
The news is welcomed like a bad dose of head lice.

I remind Sally about the sonnet I'm still owed.
She smiles, says she'll get to it after her midterm on *Hamlet*.
I'm not sure if she thinks I'm quaint or just plain odd.

I treat myself to Sancerre with my omelette.
It's been a tough day and I still have a thesis on Nelly Sachs
by a student who evidently hasn't heard of an umlaut

to get through. Bill Clinton's on TV, playing sax.
When I come to, a biopic of Tiger or Vijay
seems like the loneliest possible alternative to sex.

I'm too old for this. I feel like some hoary, washed-up hoojah
on the edge of that funfair, waiting for the carousel
to jolt into life like a wound-up hummingbird or jay

to circulate a sincere song of desire, blaze, arousal.

Horses

The drier gives the first two notes
of 'In the Bleak Midwinter'
before giving up the ghost.

The clothes horse will have to come
into its own, propped in the bath
like a newborn foal, all joints and poise,

as if sizing up the hurdle of the one blue rim
that stands before our backyard fence
and the thin-lipped creek

that skirts two fields below a road
I knew the ins and outs of when
he used to unpick his day, step by step,

flat cap and hip flask, whistling
an ascending scale that tilted,
over the top, into the ditch.

He bred horses, fenced them in clean lines,
swaddled them in cast-off woollens,
gave them our names,

walked out to stand with them
one Christmas Day; brought back
to the house a voice infused

with inland fields and breath
that flocked above them
like damp flannel, streaming silks.

By and By

Noon
shoulders
its way
through heat
like a horseman
in uniform
on a country lane
who calls
'Stay there'
to a yellow girl
lagging
some short
way behind.

Oh, my lost
father, stay;
there's a catch
of shadow
at your back
and this hour
will stand
to either
side of us,
like painted
gateposts.

Here's all
the life
I would
set out for us:
a future left
like the note
on a yellow
kitchen table
reminding you

to call
for me
on the
way home.

The Family Room

The sea loses memory
in midland shallows.
So much of what it has to say
is the sound of a small boy
in a navy jacket
running over stones,

then hunkering
under triple windows
that empty into evergreens
and seaweed drapes.

There is a shimmer
of newspaper clippings
and a red pen
that knows everything
but still needs to be told.

From here on in
light will be noiseless,
chastened, as if
holding its breath.
Ask any question
of a bolt of smoke;
the scissors will answer
'Indeed, indeed'.

The Clutch Handbag

Black bombazine with grosgrain binding,
a clasp of diamanté butterflies and a row
of bevelled ivory sequins threaded with slipknots.

Finesse. A lipstick of a certain red,
a bronze compact, the cachet
of an embossed cigarette case.

Emerald lining that is like glossy music
from a dance-hall band or the sheen
of sable eyes on the mink stole

whose snout rounds on the very shape
of a tear in the satin no bigger than
her incarnadine thumbnail

through which five decades
have slipped like small coins
skittering the opening notes

of a foxtrot or an old-time waltz
that nobody, but nobody,
recalls.

Aubade

You say that you heard piano chords rustling in the night;
that you woke once and saw me there, and again.
Then I was gone. The sea under your bed said something
like your name: you thought you'd drown.

This morning your fever slinks away
like a dog bested by the hubbub of city-fed
and workaday birdsong come into its own.
You call. You want some toast.

The trees are bone dry; sunlight hunkers behind them.
Your hair fronds when I lift your head
as if out of a sea pulling away. I offer you
the lidded cup. You take it and you drink.

Let the worst I ever do to you be die.
Turn your head sideways, dear, so I can watch you sleep.
Let the morning have us, and the afternoon.
I am here, blessed, capable of more.

Pastoral

I've ruined it.
Thirty, forty years from now,
she'll hear it again
and it won't be just
a clarinet cuckoo
in a thicket of strings
but her long-dead mother
in an apron with French cheeses on it,
turning from the sink to say,
'Listen, here it comes'.

*

The streetlamp
of my laptop flicks back on
and the automatic light upstairs
flutters two goldfish
that are the only living things
inside these walls,
not counting me.

*

Lilac buds
on his black sleeve
is how his pollen
requires me
to become
a clear night sky
in which new stars,
thousands of them,
are called upon
to bloom.

Away

I babysit by Skype,
breakfast to their lunch,
lunch to their dinner.

I straighten uniforms, ask French,
nag music practice, argue *Friends*,
trim their Bebo access.

I touch their silky faces on my screen.
I am three thousand miles ago,
five hours in the red.

What would it take —
one crossed cyber wire,
a virtual hair's breadth awry —

for these synapsed hours
to bloat to centuries,
for my background

to be rescinded
to a Botticelli blue,
my webcam image

ruffed and pearled,
speaking vintage words
into spindrift?

Or, failing that,
for me to be headlonged
into light years off

to the room of an obsolete laptop
where I Skype and Skype
and no one answers,

where I Google Earth to see
if the world namechecks
this morning

my son's bike in the garden,
my daughter's skirt
on the line?

Bodkin

A word from a dream, or several, spiked on it
like old receipts. Something akin to a clavicle's
bold airs; a measurement of antique land;
a keepsake brooch on a quilted silk bodice;
a firkin, filled to the brink with mead or milk;
a bobbin spinning like a back-road drunken bumpkin;
borrowed, half-baked prophecies in a foreign tongue;
a debunked uncle's thin bloodline; a Balkan
fairy story, all broken bones poked inside out;
a bespoke book blacked in with Indian ink;
a bobolink in a buckeye or a bare-backed oak;
a barren spindle, choked ankle-high with lichen;
a fistful of ball bearings dropped on a *bodhrán*.
Body skin. Kith and kin. Other buckled things.

The Sunroom

In the hotel lobby of a Sunday afternoon I dicker
with elsewhere. The children are going storm-wild
upstairs with two new kids from up the road.
The wine kicks in. I am listening to the spindly chords
played out by the willow's decorative, Pre-Raphaelite hands,
but that won't do. There is nothing here of stillness,
no borrowed play of narrative and flaw. My daughter
is tricksy and intent; my son, doughty and kind.
We are, in this half-hearted hour, some kind
of improbable answer to the world outside.

The sunroom is the porch of a Retirement Home.
They are all taken up, the still-alive, with the business
of buttons to be stitched on shirts, words to be mended,
postcards, roses, the tilt of a waltz, a bookie's stub
in an old prayer book, something to be grateful for,
like tea in a flask carried out to the field,
her white hand waving from the gatepost,
how loose her hair, how dark on floury shoulders
that she'd let him kiss, as a small boy would,
on early, sunlit Sundays in their room.

The sunroom is a crystal cruise ship in line
at the head of the bay. We are giddy and sunlit.
We relish how warmth pins us to our loungers
like a dress pattern to satin; satin to skin.
From the dining room of the upper floor
the small talk of silverware and cut glass wisps away.
Shouts from the open-air swimming pool are spindrift
on the deck. A fashion show kicks off in the lobby,
music tinkles downstairs like a tipsy socialite.
Someone calls out 'Mother'. Somebody laughs.

I'm through, I think, with metaphor. The sunroom
floats nowhere; there is no other version of this

set out in the garden like a picnic table at sundown
with the napkins still folded, the food untouched.
I'm wanted; they're calling from lives that don't rattle
when a wind blows so the willow spells out something
on the glass that is like a name or the co-ordinates
of a moment that spoke once, but quietly, for a whole life.
Here it is, my riff and code: a creak when I stand, a 'Yes',
a single cough as I slap shut my notebook, move away.

The Box

Nightly the open plan of this last house
pulses and contracts. We pass nights
between us, draw-strung, written on;
whole hours assigned to music that folds
them into discreet forms like origami birds.

It is not our fault that what you play
opens and closes boxes of water
like the lighthouse in your dream;
that one is lying on its side; that all
the years we lived here drain away.

Intimacy

How did the peacock feather come to be
found out in the yard, trampled, half-broken,
its wild eye tamed with dirt?

The last I saw, it was in the pewter jug
on the mantelpiece, so full of itself
the whole room bent into its good grace.

You carried it in so tenderly
across your open palms
as if it were a missive or a veil.

Lay it down there on the newspaper;
let it settle, unearth itself.
Then we will get to work.

The Stairwell

Everything that mattered to me
hauls a solemn sleep
out of this night.

I hear pitchers
lowered in the stairwell
shuffle up
under the weight
of all their easy dreams.

I hear machinery
under the eaves,
a pendulum
four storeys high
being swayed
and checked
by the rise and fall
of thin-veined,
birdcage chests.

I know someone
will have to pulley cupfuls
to spill like mercury
over these
small hours

but I also know
it will not
be me.

Rain Songs

The rain makes the world creak, unfold
like a ball of cellophane
released from the hand of one
who is miles away.

*

No let up. Eighteen days and still
the monologue of petty grievance
that is its one and only torch song
witters on.

When I sit in the car on the passenger side
wet from the sunroof drips on my blouse
so my left breast mints a coin of damp
and the nag and scold of wipers tunes in
to the squall of a newborn wanting to be fed.

*

The rain conjures right angles
out of thin air, like Bartok's violin duos
that strip the swagger from a gypsy tune
and walk it into riddles and cascade.
Ancient rain, all grimace and sequins:
it drags its tired metaphors through the yard
and does not know how to climb down
from glossy stilts that stake these waking hours.
It contradicts our every word, corners us
as if we were listening to different CDs,
calling to each other from separate rooms
across silences that don't happen at once
or the transatlantic time lag, five hours on pause,
silting so much of what there is to say.

Trapdoor

All day the water has been acquiring serenity
only to throw on an evening gown of onyx silk
and presume to be on intimate terms
with worldly hills, a knowledgeable sky.

It fools no one.
Not the dragonflies or midges,
not the pine trees or the moon,
not the swimmer, me, breaststroking out

to immerse myself at its dark heart,
to witness how nothing, not even silence
or my own dim company, can disturb
that practised and accomplished suffering.

There is a trapdoor I have seen before.
Tonight, for the life of me, I raise it up,
ease myself through, go down within the pike,
the undertow, those two young deaths,

the former dock that, one night,
simply unhinged itself and drifted back
beyond a superficial gloss
to within the lake.

The Island

'Die Todteninsel' (1890) by Max Klinger

What will become of these ghosts
in our two boats; burdensome ghosts
we have commissioned ourselves to row
by equal strokes through the here and now
of your oars scratching the ink-black
as mine, to keep time, offer back
the ins and outs of a single pulse
that we learned over years to parse
as noun and verb, as rhyme, all told,
innocent and reckless as the load
that is no load, that leaves the boats
not a whit or whisper lighter yet
for having disembarked?

Other People's Lives

That letter you promised me writes itself
in a sheaf of streets with their bar hubbub:
bottles poured onto a midden in a lane, the odd jazz riff,
a clasp of laughter, some half-shouted name.

I might as well be out on the rocks, leafing through
an archived sea for a single entry to account for
my guest metaphors; to ascribe to me some pageantry,
street hymns yeasting, nightly, within these tepid hours.

What has the measure of the all-insistent, offshore boom
of other people's lives? Not the wood pigeon that, at least
for now, has stopped clattering aloneness in the rowan.
Not the cigarette's calligraphy that has nothing to explain.

Not the halogen light that islands the deck,
pinpointing your absence in this and every night.

Orchard with Lovers

She has a dress of sequinned apples,
eyelids glossed in burnish
borrowed from the tracery
of a thousand leaves.

Gilded in afternoons,
absorbed in vermilion evenings
sworn to love,
she could be a trick of the light

except that her lover's eye steadies her
from a kindred darkness
that will vouchsafe
the outcome of desire.

For now his buckle is intimate
with the glint of her hairpin.
His shirt answers the faintest whim
of rapture in her hands.

This art makes children of them.

Though the trees sweep the sky
of the dust of centuries,
of narrow workrooms
and pointillist lamps;

though filigree streets ornament
their ends and purposes;
though the foliage shimmers
all its absolved suns,

there is no question of harm.

The light between trees
is a hall composed of screens
that close over, nightly. There
we leave them, wishful and enamoured

as the loved world asks them to be.

Six Months

APRIL

My daughter buys
her first perfume.
It's called 'One Summer'.

MAY

Geese hemstitch the wetlands:
I foretell a skittery afternoon.

JUNE

Pick up the day
by four white hours;
shake it out
over long grass.

JULY

Blue sky on the radio,
all four car windows down.
Is this what it means, then,
to have friends?

AUGUST

The jet plane
tucking up its wheels
jolts me back years

to a light cadenza's
lift-off in my womb.

SEPTEMBER

A twinge in my elbow chimes, pretty much,
with the indicator of the school bus in front
and the backbeat of whatever song
is plied on the radio.
My son knows the words.
This is my life.
Let me want nothing more.

Wind in Trees

Tonight the wind tries on fancy dress
in the attic rooms of trees,

crinolines and winkle-pickers,
mustachios and swords,

a jewelled fob-watch keeping time
with my shutters' throb and hum.

Silks crinkle precisely at my window
and, at my door, an ivory cane

is summoning my name.
I ask will anything ever change.

First the trees say 'No' to me.
Then the wind says 'Yes'.

Beyond Me

The hours stack up like saucers. The knives
are resting on their polished sides. A widening stream
from the back-door light is the last thing sure of itself.

Rain falls in reams: whatever else there is allays
a loneliness plump with your absence, that balances,
tightrope and fall, to either side of me.

What do I ask? To make something of these lines
extend to you; to have you turn in my direction;
the long-life bulb by my front door illuminate your hand.

Even a single hair on your pillow knows all there is of you:
even more than I, though I have thought of you,
made much of your fern eyes and speckled wrist

and another life that barely fronts on mine.
Yet I will press a version of you between
unyielding sheets. Here is one element:

the world means more to me because you're in it.
You settle beyond me and I can rest too,
lay myself down and leave the sun

and outstretched trees alone.
They can find their own way
while I tinker with knives and hours

and one strand of your hair.
I have nothing to ask.
It is not over. I will not again.

Desire

I would like
to feel indifferent
as a plinth or tabletop
of pure Carrara marble
that has all its darkness
corralled in veins
that hold themselves
instinctively intact.

*

But his name
is a coin flipped
in a clearing
at the dead centre
of wherever I am.

*

And the skin between
his thigh and hip
comes between me
and sleep.

*

I am long enough flirting
with purchase and perch.
I will set myself down, white feather,
on the world's wide open palm.

Texts

An oyster opens wide at full moon.
— Leonardo da Vinci

If there were ever words that knew of love
what could be done: wrap them in sunlight
or give them footsteps that are only, in fact,
rain falling from leaves? Swaddle them on a rib
or a skiff afloat an open moon; send them ahead
like a text to alight on a new lover's mobile?

A dazzle of minnows in a rock pool might be
as close to love; a metaphor no more significant
or marked than the openings that spindrift makes
when it falls back on the sea. Or that rain makes:
every drop coining a selfsame moon as that phone's
initial zero. Or the centre of a love affair,
a clearing where the response lands, disclosing
in its silver ringtone, one silver disclosure.

Inside Out

All the indoor years,
various fires, bar counters, polished words,
the rooms of summer opening on each other

I would turn out, warm ash and cinder,

to scatter over a bend in the road
that opens on the lit window
where I almost am.

*

I remember white tulips I had once,
how they faced down
an opaque, bathroom wall
to arrive at a semblance of light.

*

Put down the moonlight on the tablecloth.
I want to kiss your mouth.

*

What good is all this nightly rain
if not to be made a pillow of
to slip beneath your head?

*

Take a brace of conifers
as though it were a bolt of cloth
of black and olive green and cutwork stars
with sky-blue beads between the tips
of branches, overall.

Pull it close around us.
We'll sleep underneath.

Love Songs

Your email shimmers
in my inbox.

Here are your words,
inestimable, smooth
to my fingertip,
as though, by touch,
they could be made
to open a chink more.

*

I would have you lie down
on young heather,
all the years between us
pressed clean like sheets of linen,
and everything that might have been
come round again
as the sea worn
on your wrists.

*

The bruise on my forearm
puts me in mind
of the hole in your sleeve
through which I would,
if so allowed,
sieve every waking hour.

*

The flare of the mobile phone
in my hand
is an outcrop of sunlight

in which we sit
eavesdropping the gossip
of bracken and fern
while I watch your freckles ripen
to the same shade
as my own.

*

What will I do
when I am too old
for such love songs?

An Teach Tuí

Thistledown, fuchsia, flagstone floor:
this noun house

has the wherewithal
to sit out centuries,

squat between bog-water darkness
and rooms turned inside out to summer,

straw-coloured months of childhood
answering each other

like opposite windows in thickset walls
that sunlight will cajole.

Tea roses bluster the half-door.
Rain from eaves footfalls the gravel.

A robin, cocksure of himself,
frittered away all morning in the shrub.

If I knew how to fix in even one language
the noise of his wings in flight

I wouldn't need another word.

Derryloughane

Weaver's Hill anchors this evening.
Tomorrow it will haul itself off
to a future packed deep, as cargo,
in emeralds and jade,

but tonight it broods, implacable,
just north of our rooflines

and all the ropes that tether it
end in earthed limestone
that has in it the glaze and theatre
of a Japanned sky.

Rummy

Two moons vying in angled glass cast doubt
over a rummy hand of sequences and sets.
August has been fanning itself on the deckchair.
I could sit for whole, plump hours there
waiting for some sign of my return
and an ocean and a road could wait with me,
a field of scrub, two telegraph poles,
a wall in fits and starts, and cars shook out,
like greyhounds, from a sly turn in the road.
A moth flickers in out of one half of the night:
there are months to be got through now.
I play three kings and a run from the four.
Until the next time. Bring summer back:
two moons with a hill between them
will be holding out for you.

The High Room

Who paints the ocean
as a small boy running,
the islands as a pebble
skimmed from his hand?

Who drapes a tablecloth
of cloud over Weaver's Hill;
opens a cutwork metal screen
behind mackerel rocks?

The blue path loses ground.
Over the mantelpiece of Clare
a study of the painter's family
plays draughts with whole moons.

The Difficult Poem

No problem can be solved from the same level of consciousness that created it.

The August that finds me
in a gifted cottage
with maroon windows
and a fuchsia half-door

leads me to believe
Einstein was right.

I have already forgone
my book on bliss.

Next to go is a poem
about *ogham* stitches
on a suicide's wrist

in favour of
a 30-minute cassette,
Christmas Music 1998.

The Huddersfield Choral Society Youth Choir's
'Joy to the World'
does for the rusty-hinged donkey bray.

'Silent Night' resolves the issue
of summertipsy dusk

and midges swarm
amid winter's snow.

What was the problem
with that sonnet
about rain in the sycamore?

It centered on my use of ‘froth’.
That is all I can remember.

Pier

Speak to our muscles of a need for joy.
— W H Auden, 'Sonnets from China' (XVII)

Left at the lodge and park, snout to America.
Strip to togs, a shouldered towel, flip-flop over
the tarmac past the gangplanked rooted barge,
two upended rowboats and trawlers biding time.
Nod to a fisherman propped on a bollard,
exchange the weather, climb the final steps
up to the ridge. And then let fly. Push wide,
tuck up your knees so the blue nets hold you,
wide-open, that extra beat. Gulp cloud;
fling a jet trail round your neck like a feather boa,
toss every bone and sinew to the plunge.
Enter the tide as if it were nothing,
really nothing, to do with you. Kick back.
Release your ankles from its coiled ropes;
slit water, drag it open, catch your breath.
Haul yourself up into August. Do it over,
raucously. Head first. This time, shout.

The Penknife

One slip and the tip
of my forefinger slits
inch-wide, clean-brimmed
so a flap of skin
is mackerel-gilled,
ripped white to the rim
like the single thread
that pulls open a wave
to a skim of pulse,
a spate of blood and salt.

Power Cut

I have extravagant fire, two candles bottled in last summer's vintage,
a magazine with pictures of gold dresses. I hardly can make out the words.
The wind talks up small hours, shakes out huge white sheets against the night.
Headlamps shuffle gates and gateposts, throw up slabs of indigo on windows,
happen on a snatch of stone, an angled roof, a single telegraph pole. Worlds
turn themselves inside out: rooms flood with darkness; roads funnel light.

My mobile baubles now and then. Otherwise, mute as a sod of turf,
it squats on the mantelpiece. I might as well be a remnant envoy
to a province of depleted relevance, outlying home. I am too much me.
A full moon hangs in the balance. Am I nothing without love?

Purism

The wind orchestrates
its theme of loneliness
and the rain
has too much glitter in it, yes.

They are like words, the wrong ones,
insisting I listen to sense.
But I too am obstinate.

I have white walls,
white curtained windows.
What need have I
of the night's jet-black,
outlandish ornament?

What I am after
is silence
in proportion
to desire,

the way music plumbs
its surfaces
as straight words do
the air between them.

I begin to learn
the simple thing

burning through
to an impulse at once lovely
and given to love

that will not be refused.

Cowslips

Four times I have thrust my writing hand
into a tuft of cowslips:
once, for starters, in the ditches of childhood,
years later, in a book of Dürer prints,
and then in a Washington gallery, for real,
where I found it proved no more vivid, or less,
than what is growing beside me now in a pot
on my patio. To my left, cowslips;
to my right, a print of cowslips
dislodged from clay and context
except for the vellum's wash of earth
that is a kind of framing device as definite
as these straight and straightforward lines.

Drawn, as it were, on both a horizontal
and a vertical scale, an ardour of leaves
pushing east and west, even out to the margin
of brown ink that squares up to the limits of art.
The leaves are decades, centuries,
each with its own delineation
that matters not a whit. The leaves
are how we live every day, how we spread
a green, embroidered cloth over waking hours.

The flowers are emergence, the flare
of dim brilliance by which we mark our time.
The flowers love the world, have reason to:
they are aspirant, barely beautiful, almost soaked
into the background of golden, besmirched air
that is, always, a morning in 1526
stippling the seal of gouache
to interrupt accomplishment
with creases and the finest cracks
that might be said to breathe;
and are yet discernible as slight rebuke

to years lived in between
as if there were no such cowslips
to be given to such light.

I know it now. I have asked the question
of a flower or print I always lacked the guts
to ask of life. I thought it would be cowslips always,
tufts of them seedling all over my time.

And it has been.

I mean, it was.

Spindrift

for Tommy and Eve

1

What is to be done
with a past tense
that, once recalled,
presents itself again?

You might as well
throw a stone in the sea
and be taken aback
when the same thing
is keeping you from sleep.

2

Two floors above sea level,
two narrow windows, two broad.

A sandstone fireplace jiggers, nightly,
card games and small hours,
all manner of old news.

3

Telephone wires
traipse the field
where we drew water
to gloss over months away,
left a rock with twine around it
and a path to keep track of
the goings on of every stone

and high-wire lament
the hill sent down to us.

4

We unpack,
make up the beds.
I light a fire
with last year's turf.

5

The colour of the sea today
is nothing like the name
of any colour
I can think of.

6

The field
is silked
in magenta.
Ragwort
sequins it.

7

I drink tea
from a yellow mug
that is as old as I am.

8

Heather and willowherb,
clover and vetch,
gentians, buttercups,
stone.

9

Honeycomb fields.
Low clouds
swarm over them.

10

It is what it is:
a yellow field
with four halved eggs
well-stayed and handkerchiefed.

11

A deckchair
drifting out to sea
in the lawn's long grass.

12

Hide and seek
in the windbreak.
I never grew out of it.

13

They're waving
at drivers
coming down
the road,

keeping up
a running count
of how many
wave back.

14

Where is that
currach going
and where is it
coming from?

15

Cyclists surge headlong
into brush-stroked
cottages and clouds.

16

Another football
lost to the furze;
wait for winter
to retrieve it.

17

The turn in the boreen
down to the shore
sunlight takes
in its stride.

18

So much sky:
you'd think
the sheer heft of it
would eventually
wear thin.

19

A wave opens
on the bay
like a lifted thread
in a canvas flat
already primed
indigo.

20

All horizontals:
stone walls, the road,
an ocean stretched out
like an artist's model
on a hotel chaise,
all lace and gravitas.

21

Tilted up at one corner,
the bay would spill
into my whole life.

22

Between the headland
and the island
a skylight opens
as the shutter
in 'French Window at Nice'.

23

The sea's mood
swivels on a sixpence
thrown in off the rocks
Augusts ago
by a girl who has been
fingering it since.

24

The waves break a cleaner white
than the Planning Application
fixed to the gatepost.

25

The future tense
of the bracken stream
coming down
off the hill
is a water feature
in a landscaped garden
fringed with exotic fern.

26

A field of scrub
might yield a bicycle,
a bungalow,
even roses,
given time.

27

There is only now
to toss around
like a small word
in an empty box,
a single, low-slung
rain cloud
gaining on
the bay.

28

All morning
foostering
in the wings;
with the evening news,
the rain's last
curtain call.

29

A car from Spiddal
rounds the bend.

Rain sprays off the tyres
like blacksmith's glitz.

30

Word blackens
the coastline:
the mackerel
are in.

31

Not left on the rocks,
not cast in the sea,
that bladed pollock head.

The murk of the rock pool
suddens with fresh red.

32

Clouds soak the foreshore,
foam shoals over Moher.

33

When a blackberry gives
up its roadside perch
and squats, all dainty, in my grasp,
all that is left for me
is to try to gauge how sweet it is
and not assume a bitterness
that will smear my tongue
prodigious black.

34

Bog cotton, convolvulus,
cow parsley, woodbine;
the whitewashed
gable wall
sees off
the lot.

35

An archipelago
of lit windows
drifts past
our moored
lookout.

36

The island lighthouse
clenches the bay
and then sets it free.

37

Awash with headlights,
the blue room
passes through
the wake
of closing time.

38

All night the sea chatters to itself:
a hundred different escapades
with the same punchline.

39

Headlights from Furbo,
streetlamps in Vienna;
rain on the window,
Klimt's luminous orchard.

40

Ghosts tinkling in the bedroom
fall silent when we turn in.

41

Down on the rocks
a driftwood moon
is whitening
tonight.

42

Each morning
to be cornflowered;
each night-time
to be greened over
in scutch and fern,
wild sorrel.

43

Even the road knows
what I know of the world.

The wall and shore, chimney and sky,
lean into the good of it.

44

My answer blooms
like shingle
I am dusting now
between my fingertips.

45

It is all a kind
of love song, really,
and I am only
listening to it,
trying to follow
the words.

Acknowledgements and Notes

Thanks are due to the editors of the following publications in which these poems, or versions of them, have appeared: *The Antioch Review, Areté, Blackbox Manifold, Free Verse, The Indiana Review, The Irish Times, The Kenyon Review, The Manchester Review, Oxfam Calendar 2009, PN Review, Poetry, Poetry Ireland Review, Poetry London, Poetry Northwest, Poetry Review, Ropes, The SHOp, Smartish Pace, Sunday Miscellany* (RTÉ), *Times Literary Supplement, Wasafiri* and *The Yale Review.*

Thanks to the Arts Council of Ireland for a Bursary in Literature (2008-09). Thanks also to Dr Pat Donlon and the staff of the Tyrone Guthrie Centre at Annaghmakerrig for unfailing hospitality.

page 13 *Mo Cheol Thú.* A Sunday morning Irish music programme presented by Ciarán MacMathúna on RTÉ radio from 1970 to 2005.

page 50 *An Teach Tuí* translates as 'The Thatched House'.